W9-AZZ-963

Ancient Rome

by Lucia Raatma

Content Adviser: Michael Danti, Ph.D., Research Specialist,
Near East Section, University of Pennsylvania Museum, Philadelphia

Reading Adviser: Dr. Linda D. Labbo, Department of Reading Education,
College of Education, The University of Georgia

Let's See Library
Compass Point Books
Minneapolis, Minnesota

Compass Point Books
151 Good Counsel Drive
P.O. Box 669
Mankato, MN 56002-0669

Copyright © 2003 by Compass Point Books
All rights reserved. No part of this book may be reproduced without written permission
from the publisher. The publisher takes no responsibility for the use of any of the materials
or methods described in this book, nor for the products thereof.
Printed in the United States of America.

 This book was manufactured with paper containing
at least 10 percent post-consumer waste.

Cover: Colosseum, Rome, Italy

Photographs ©: Dallas and John Heaton/Corbis, cover; Stock Montage, 6, 14, 18, 20; North Wind Picture
Archives, 8, 10, 12, 16.

Editors: E. Russell Primm, Emily J. Dolbear, and Pam Rosenberg
Photo Researcher: Svetlana Zhurkina
Photo Selector: Linda S. Koutris
Designer: Melissa Voda
Cartographer: XNR Productions, Inc.

Library of Congress Cataloging-in-Publication Data
Raatma, Lucia.
    Ancient Rome / by Lucia Raatma.
        p. cm. — (Let's see library)
    Summary: Describes the history, government, people, culture, aspects of daily life, and enduring legacy of
ancient Rome. Includes bibliographical references and index.
    ISBN 978-0-7565-0292-8 (hardcover)
    ISBN 978-0-7565-2278-0 (paperback)
        1. Rome—Civilization—Juvenile literature. [1. Rome—Civilization.] I. Title. II. Series.
    DG77 .R16 2002
    937—dc21   2002003040

Visit Compass Point Books on the Internet at *www.compasspointbooks.com*
or e-mail your request to *custserv@compasspointbooks.com*

Table of Contents

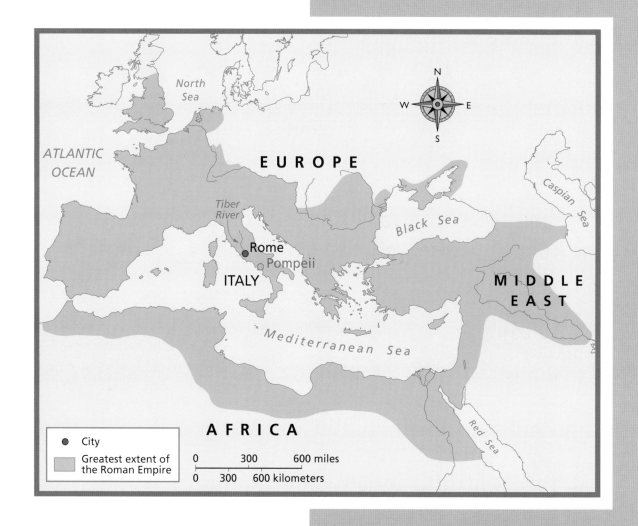

North Sea

ATLANTIC OCEAN

EUROPE

Tiber River

Rome
Pompeii

ITALY

Black Sea

Caspian Sea

MIDDLE EAST

Mediterranean Sea

Red Sea

AFRICA

• City

Greatest extent of the Roman Empire

0   300   600 miles
0   300   600 kilometers

What Was Ancient Rome?

Palatine Hill is one of seven hills along the Tiber River. The Tiber River runs into the Tyrrhenian Sea. There, a little village began as a farming community. This is where the city of Rome was started around 753 B.C. A famous story tells that twin brothers named Romulus and Remus founded the city of Rome.

Over hundreds of years, the city grew to become the Roman **Empire**. That empire included all of Italy and about half of Europe. It also included the northern part of Africa and a large part of the Middle East.

◀ *The city of Rome was the center of the Roman Empire.*

Who Were the Ancient Romans?

Some ancient Romans were more important than others. Members of government and their families were in this important group. Rich people who owned land were also included. Most other people were farmers and soldiers. Some people were slaves.

In Rome, men and women wore simple clothes called tunics. Men wore togas over their tunics. Togas and tunics were draped over the Romans' bodies like big sheets. Men's clothing was usually white, but upper-class men often had a purple border on their togas.

◄ *An ancient Roman soldier holds a spear and shield.*

What Kind of Daily Life Did They Have?

Wealthy Romans lived in large houses with many **servants**. They enjoyed big meals. They ate vegetables with meat or fish, and sweet cakes for dessert. People in the city lived in crowded apartment buildings. Country people lived in small houses. These working-class Romans usually ate bread, fruit, and cheese.

Roman families were usually large. Most children were taught at home by their parents. Children from wealthy families went to school when they were older. There they studied Latin, mathematics, public speaking, and music.

◀ *Wealthy Romans often had big houses with fancy gardens.*

What Was the Religion of Ancient Rome?

In ancient Rome, most people worshiped several gods and goddesses. Jupiter was the god of the sky. He was the most important god to the Romans. Ceres was the goddess of farming and the harvest. Venus was the goddess of love, while Mars was the god of war. Diana was the goddess of hunting. The Romans built temples to honor these gods.

Over time, the Romans became interested in other religions. Some Romans became Christians. The Christians often faced brutal cruelty in ancient Rome.

◄ *A mask of Jupiter, the Roman god of the sky*

What Did Romans Do for Fun?

The people of ancient Rome enjoyed holidays. On holidays they often went to events at the Colosseum. The Colosseum was a large outdoor theater. Some violent games took place there. Men called **gladiators** battled each other until one of them died. At **chariot** races, the crowds cheered for the drivers.

Public bathhouses were popular places to relax. There people bathed in steam baths and indoor pools.

◄ Chariot races took place at the Circus Maximus and other large arenas.

What Kind of Government Did They Have?

In the beginning, Rome was ruled by kings. These kings worked with members of the **Senate** to make laws. Roman citizens could meet and vote on the laws. Only men could be citizens, though.

In 27 B.C. that system changed. The Roman **Republic** became the Roman Empire. The king was replaced by an emperor. The emperors did not work well with the Senate. Citizens had little control over the government. Many of the emperors were very powerful. They helped the Roman Empire become very large.

◄ *Julius Caesar was a famous Roman general and leader. He was killed in 44 B.C.*

What Kind of Work Did They Do?

Most people in ancient Rome were farmers. They grew wheat, barley, grapes, and olives. They raised sheep, goats, pigs, and other animals. Children often worked on the family farms.

Roman merchants **imported** food, silk, ivory, and other goods. Also, mines throughout the empire produced marble, gold, and silver. Roman ships carried all these goods down huge rivers and across the Mediterranean Sea.

Some ancient Romans worked in the Forum. This area was the center of the city of Rome. It included markets, temples, and government buildings.

◄ *The Forum was a busy place at the center of the city of Rome.*

What Arts Were Important in Ancient Rome?

Architecture was important in ancient Rome. Roman buildings often had arches, covered walkways, and large courtyards. The Romans invented concrete. This material helped them build strong walls.

Romans enjoyed poetry and plays. One famous poem, the *Aeneid*, tells the story of Rome. It was written by the poet Virgil.

Painting and sculpture were important to the Romans. Large wall paintings decorated the homes of the wealthy. Many statues showed famous people or historical events.

◀ *The Pantheon was a temple in ancient Rome. It was rebuilt in the second century and still stands today.*

How Do We Remember Ancient Rome?

We remember Rome as a mighty empire. Many modern farmers still use ideas from Roman farms. Some modern governments are based on the Roman system. Designs for Roman bridges, roads, and **aqueducts** are often studied when modern ones are built.

We have learned about Rome through written records, paintings, and statues. Roman towns and cities have taught us a lot. The city of Pompeii was buried when a nearby volcano erupted. Scientists uncovered this city and others. All these things teach us about life in ancient Rome.

◄ *The Colosseum can still be seen by visitors in the modern city of Rome.*

Glossary

aqueducts—large bridges built to carry water across a valley

architecture—designing buildings

chariot—a two-wheeled cart pulled by horses

empire—several countries ruled by the same government

gladiators—fighters who battled each other or wild animals until one of them died

imported—brought in from another place

republic—a government that allows citizens to elect representatives

Senate—the supreme council of ancient Rome

servants—people who take care of the household chores and personal needs of others

Did You Know?

• The Roman's name for the Mediterranean Sea was *Mare Nostrum*. These Latin words mean "Our Sea."

• The city of Rome was the largest city in the Roman Empire. At one point, ancient Rome was home to almost 1 million people.

• Many of the Roman gods were similar to the Greek gods. They just had different names.